'Volunteer!'
The Lancashire Rifle Volunteers
1859–1885

'Volunteer!': The Lancashire Rifle Volunteers
by Stephen Bull

Text copyright © Lancashire County Museums Service, 1993

Published by Lancashire County Books, 143 Corporation Street, Preston

Typeset by Carnegie Publishing Ltd., 18 Maynard Street, Preston

Printed by Pindar Graphics (Preston) Ltd., 1 Garstang Rd, Preston

British Library Cataloguing-in-Publication Data
A CIP record for this book is available from the British Library.

ISBN 1-871236-25-8

Acknowledgements

THIS BOOKLET was first produced to accompany an exhibition on Lancashire's volunteers held at the County and Regimental Museum at Preston.

In addition to those persons and institutions noted in the picture captions the author would especially like to thank the Library, Museum and Arts Committee of Lancashire County Council; the County Employers Liaison Team of the TAVR; Mr John Blundell, County Museums Officer; Lt Col A. Rigby; Board of Trustees of the National Museums and Galleries on Merseyside (King's Regimental Collection) (especially Peter Grey); Blackburn Museum; the Loyal North Lancashire Regiment Museum; the South Lancashire Regiment Museum; the Lancashire Fusiliers Museum; the Liverpool Scottish Museum; Lancaster City Museum; Museum of the Manchester Regiment; Mr H. Wilkinson; Mr M. Seed; Lt Col A. L. M. Cook, Mr F. Read; Mr S. Eastwood; Mr R. Westlake; Mrs S. Hopkins, National Army Museum; and numerous members of staff of both the Lancashire County and Manchester libraries.

Thanks are due to the Board of Trustees of the National Museums and Galleries on Merseyside (King's Regimental Collection) for permission to reproduce the watercolour of the members of the 80th (Liverpool) 'Press Guard' on page 13 and the photograph of Private Jamieson of the 15th (Liverpool) L.R.V. on page 28; and to the King's Own Royal Regimental Museum, Lancaster for permission to reproduce the photograph of the unidentified officer of the 10th (Lancaster) L.R.V. on page 7 and the 'orders of dress' on page 31.

The cover illustration is a detail of a painting by Wladimir Sherwood depicting the laying of the foundation stone of Blackburn Exchange, 1863. It shows Captain Thomas Lund in front of the 2nd (Blackburn) LRV who are in the act of firing a volley into the air. The painting is held at Blackburn Museum and Art Gallery, and is reproduced with the kind permission of the museum.

*Captain Nathanial G. P. Bousfield in the uniform of the 1st (Liverpool) L.R.V.,
c. 1860. Bousfield's sword is preserved in the King's Liverpool Regiment Collection.
(Courtesy of Col A. L. M. Cook.)*

Origins of the Rifle Volunteers

AFTER THE NAPOLEONIC WARS ended on the field of Waterloo in 1815 there was peace in Europe and little possibility of England being invaded in the foreseeable future. Yet by the late 1840s all this had changed; there were revolutions on the continent and international tension was rising. In 1852 Devonshire offered to raise volunteers, followed shortly by London. At the same time Nathaniel Bousfield, a Liverpool cotton merchant, and twenty like-minded gentlemen began to drill and take an interest in training for citizen soldiers. Two years later, when the Crimean War broke out and the Liverpool Drilling Club was officially formed, there were over a hundred in the ranks.

It would, however, take a worse crisis for the government generally to accept volunteer units. In 1857 the Commander-in-Chief of the Army, the Duke of Cambridge, wrote to the secretary of state for war begging him not to entertain the idea of volunteers: 'I hope you will on no account give way to Volunteer Corps of which I see so much in the newspapers. They are unmanageable bodies and would ruin our army.' They were, in short, 'an armed and a very dangerous rabble'.

The catalyst which did change government policy was tension between Britain and France combined with increased public opinion in favour of volunteers. Early in 1858 Italian conspirators led by Felice Orsini made an attempt on the lives of Napoleon III of France and the empress on their way to the opera. Bombs were thrown and, although they were unhurt, others were killed and wounded. The immediate objective of the plotters was a free and united Italy, but Orsini had British connections, and Anglo–French relations deteriorated.

In 1859 France and Austria went to war in Italy; and the French and their Piedmontese allies won swift victories at Magenta and Solferino. The Austrians were driven out of Lombardy and Prussia began to mobilise. Europe appeared to be on the brink of a general war.

Though this cataclysm was to be averted by the treaty of Villafranca, the scare was enough to encourage France to build up her fleet and Lord Palmerston, the British prime minister, to begin a massive coastal fort-building programme, later to become known as 'Palmerston's follies'. On the continental side of the Channel many regiments in the French army passed resolutions imploring Napoleon to allow them to 'seek out and chastise' the British who had harboured the would-be assassins.

In truth the French had no invasion plan, but the political situation combined with the new technology of steam ships, ironclads and improved artillery made such a plan appear feasible. One immediate result was a clamour in the British press to increase the power of the army by accepting volunteer units to defend home shores. In *The Times* Lord Ranelagh, Major Richards, Hans Busk, Sir Duncan McDougal and others waged a campaign for recognition. On 9 May Lord Tennyson lent weight by the publication of a poem.

> There is a sound of thunder afar,
> Storm of battle and thunder of war,
> Well if it do not roll our way,
> Storm! Storm! Riflemen form!
> Ready, be ready to meet the Storm!
> Riflemen, riflemen, riflemen form!

This agitation was also taken up in the papers of the North West and more than one advert was placed asking for men interested in forming 'rifle clubs' which could subsequently be the basis of a 'rifle corps'. On 12 May 1859 Lord Derby's government took the cheapest solution to popular demands and bowed to the formation of volunteer units. In a circular issued by the secretary of state for war, persons who could furnish their own arms and equipment and 'defray all expenses' were asked to come forward. The volunteers were to be of several sorts: light horse, artillery, engineers and mounted rifles: but by far the largest bulk were the dismounted rifle volunteers.

The county rifle volunteer corps were now numbered in national order of precedence according to the sequence in which they had offered their services. Devonshire first, Middlesex (including Greater London) second and Lancashire third. Over ninety others followed, covering the whole country from Sutherland to Cornwall. By 1864 the total number of enrolled volunteers would be 170,544 and Lancashire would have one of the largest contingents.

Raising Lancashire's Rifle Volunteers

NATHANIEL BOUSFIELD was once described by a contemporary as having a 'military air, and a soul above cotton broking, smart in appearance, erect as a grenadier, an enthusiast in his chosen vocation, affable in manners and very popular'. As early as April 1859 a mass meeting had been held in Liverpool to gain support for the volunteer movement and Bousfield was aided by a petition to the government by Sir Duncan MacDougal. In May, when volunteers were officially recognised, the offer to raise a unit in Liverpool was repeated and accepted. Nathaniel Bousfield became Lancashire's first commissioned rifle volunteer officer on 11 June 1859, and the unit he had raised the 1st (Liverpool) Lancashire Rifle Volunteers. On 15 June they marched, 180 strong, to a civic reception at the Liverpool Exchange, to the sound of the national anthem.

Though being a volunteer could prove expensive, it did have the advantage that one was exempt from service in the regular army or militia. According to the War Office notice issued on 12 May 1859, volunteers were expected to attend eight drills in four months or do a total of twenty-four days' training per year to be returned as effectives. The basic organisational unit was a company with a minimum of sixty and a maximum of one hundred men commanded by a captain, aided by a lieutenant and an ensign.

Companies followed thick and fast from all over the country and the county. Feelings ran high, and fear of French invasion was one of the main motivating factors, as may be judged from a speech made to potential volunteers at Ulverston.

What is to prevent a French corvette from sailing up to Barrow and taking possession of the harbour and railway? Perhaps the last friendly and English message the Ulverstonians would have . . . would be that the French had taken possession of the hotel, that they were drinking all the light wines, that our friend Mr Ramsden was dangling by the neck to the station lamp post and in a very short time Ulverston was to be sacked and pillaged.

Soon virtually every town was to boast at least one volunteer unit. It is interesting to note how closely the procedure of forming companies followed the example set by Liverpool. In Preston a meeting was held at the town hall on 30 May 1859 and, on a motion proposed by Mr John Cooper and seconded by Mr E. Pedder, it was resolved to form a volunteer corps for

'The Borough of Preston and its Neighbourhood'. Enrolment took place in October 1859 at the militia storehouse near the prison, and subscriptions were raised. The first drill took place in November by the corn exchange. The original Preston Corps, the 11th, soon absorbed the other two; the 12th and the shortlived 30th (Fishwick).

At Wigan the original meeting to discuss raising a unit was called by the mayor, Henry Woodcock, and took place on 20 May. By November of 1859 subscriptions totalling £460 had been raised and a group of thirty men was being drilled by Police Sergeant W. Swallow at the Eagle room in the Royal Hotel. An age limit of eighteen to forty years was quickly imposed, with a minimum height requirement of five feet five inches. Not long after, the police drill instructor was replaced by Sergeant W. Bryant of the Coldstream Guards, and the drill place was moved out of doors to the grammar school yard.

In the case of Bolton, an initial meeting at Little Bolton town hall resolved not only to raise a corps but set an ambitious subscription target of £1,000. A portentous advertisement followed.

> It is particularly requested that persons of all classes, of good character, who are desirous of joining in the present movement to form a Volunteer Corps in Bolton in accordance with the terms contained in General Peel's circular of the 12th May and 25th May last, would at once communicate their names, addresses and occupations to Mr Bailey, 14 Wood Street, Bolton.

By the end of July the main sponsors of the Bolton movement had emerged as Major Pilsworth, James Watkins and Arthur Bailey. Although subscriptions were still short of the figure agreed, the project proceeded, encouraged by the news that the government was considering a subsidy for weapons.

A new meeting on 12 October was attended by Captain Gray MP, who acted as chairman, Majors Langshaw and Pilsworth, George Piggot, Arthur Bailey 'and about a dozen of the gentlemen volunteers'. Captain Hobbs of the 45th (Nottinghamshire) Regiment came to inspect the ground which had been offered to the movement by the Earl of Bradford. He declared it unsuitable and a new site was selected.

In the meantime the 'gentlemen volunteers' were not to be discouraged; they met at the grammar school and 'drilled vigorously' under the eye of Sergeant-Major Jones until a permanent meeting place could be found. The first thirty-three members of the 27th (Bolton) LRV were finally sworn in at Little Bolton town hall on 15 November. Drilling now moved to the cattle market and Lum's factory; a house in Crook Street was subsequently rented

NCOs of various Lancashire Rifle Volunteer Corps at Fleetwood, c. 1860. Notice the variety of uniforms and the muzzle-loading Enfield rifles.

as headquarters. Over much of the county the same things were happening. Inaugural meetings concluded with motions to raise volunteers, consideration was then given to funding, drilling and arming.

There were times when things did not go so smoothly, and in places there was opposition. In Rochdale and Oldham, for example, speakers branded the volunteer movement a 'Tory device' for leading the public away from the ticklish matters of reform and taxation. 'Tory device' or not, few of the original volunteers saw their motivation as party political and, in fact, more of the early supporters of the volunteers in parliament were Liberal than Conservative. Later the position reversed, and the volunteer cause became more closely linked with the Tories. After 1861 there was a deliberate effort to separate the volunteers from politics; they were forbidden to meet or drill at election time, and the wearing of uniform was not allowed at other than military gatherings.

In many places political opposition was less of a threat than the fact that an initial burst of enthusiasm would be followed by lethargy or a cold realisation of the expense of the undertaking. In Ramsbottom there was difficulty raising the necessary sixty men for the minimum size company, and nowhere could be found for drill or storage of weapons; it was therefore some time before the 57th LRV could be organised.

In the 5th (Liverpool) there was a storm over restriction put on membership. A ballot box had been provided by which undesirable recruits could be 'black-balled' and excluded by the existing members. The box was smashed by one of the lieutenants and his supporters.

Money was the root of problems at Ulverston; here it was resolved first that a subscription should be raised, and then that those who were able to provide their own uniform should decide how much should be paid by the remainder.

> The latter strongly objected as being opposed to that spirit of equality, which they had been given to understand pervaded the Corps. As no attention was paid to this protest, a considerable number left the room. Snow lay on the ground and the dissenters waited outside and gave expression to their indignation by snow-balling their comrades as they left the assembly rooms. This was not by any means a hopeful beginning . . .

In other places units petered out after a while simply through waning interest. Such was the fate of the 75th (Broughton) LRV, which was extinguished in 1863 through lack of members. The record is incomplete, but it is likely that this reason underlies the disappearance of three or four other Lancashire units in the mid-1860s.

Very often officers were initially elected by their men. This was surprisingly democratic in an age of less-than-universal franchise, but choice was practically limited by the fact that being a rifle volunteer officer was both expensive and time consuming. On other occasions noblemen or industrialists put themselves forward for leadership and were able to maintain their authority and position largely by paying the expenses of others in a manner that harked back to the volunteer movement of the Napoleonic era.

In Warrington the connection with earlier wars was more tangible. The appeal for volunteers was couched in terms of reviving the spirit of the old 'bluebacks' or Royal Warrington Volunteers who had been formed in 1798, the 'Year of Liberty', when the French had invaded Ireland. In the words of a contemporary ditty aimed at Warringtonians.

> Sons of the 'Bluebacks', arouse your slumber
> To the Quakers and Cotton Lords never give heed,
> Choose ye the bravest men of your numbers
> Not objectors to die, but certain to bleed.

Incredibly, one of the main sponsors of the 9th (Warrington) LRV was John Clare, an octogenarian veteran of the original volunteers of 1798. He declared stoutly that as long as he 'could stand on his feet' and had 'a penny in his pocket', the queen, constitution and country would never lack support. He died about a year later. At more than one event Clare wore his old regimentals, but, much to his dismay, 'the uniform that fitted the young Clare so well some fifty years before was now found to fit him nowhere, and consequently Mr Greenway [the tailor] had the problem set before him of making this valued relic of the close of the previous century "pass muster" '.

Although volunteer officers were not immediately accorded the sort of status that regulars enjoyed, the social cachet of being a rifle volunteer officer should not be underestimated. The queen herself endorsed the volunteer movement by the holding of a 'levee' for officers at St James' on 7 March 1860. Doubtless many Lancashire men attended; one who definitely did was Ensign T. H. Kirkham of the 33rd (Ardwick) LRV who recorded the event in his diary. Balls were also popular: there were many, but a particularly splendid one was held at the Furness Abbey Hotel on 19 December 1860. The room was decorated with trophies

Unidentified officer of the 10th (Lancaster) L.R.V., February 1861. The cap badge of bugle horn over Lancashire rose is just visible on the forage cap.
(King's Own Museum, Lancaster.)

of arms, flowers and the monogram of the local marquis; the glittering evening attracted 'all the beauty and grace of the district'.

At least some of the 'other ranks' were also gentlemen and so it was not unexpected that they should mingle with officers at events such as plays or pantomimes put on by their companies, or that they should meet at band concerts or fund-raising bazaars. Such familiarity would, however, have been unheard of in the regulars, as John Snooks, writing to the *Examiner and Times*, remarked in August 1859.

On Sunday morning I was not a little astonished to meet two of the Manchester Rifle Corps walking in the suburbs of the City in full uniform, one of whom was dressed as an officer, the other as a private. Now, I should like to be informed if it is not contrary to all rules of military etiquette for an officer and a private to be taking a stroll together in uniform, and whether it is to be understood by the public that our gentlemen defenders are to be at liberty to don uniform and show off their handsome figures whenever they have a mind so to do. Surely there is no need for such a display of military enthusiasm, on Sunday especially, in a time of peace . . .

The 'volunteer dinner' was another perk of the club which caused considerable merriment in the press. Correspondents asked whether rifle volunteers were to be issued with spoons as well as bayonets and offered to re-christen the 6th (Manchester) LRV 'the first Manchester Volunteer Diners'. One wit placed a spoof advertisement in the *Manchester Guardian* offering for sale '50 suits of uniform, good as new, except for the Port Wine stains'. The address he gave was similar, but not identical, to that of the 6th (Manchester) LRV.

It was very noticeable that, whilst membership was theoretically open to all, in practice a larger proportion of the volunteers sprang from the middle classes than would have been true of a random cross-section of society. Mr J. Thompson junior, casting his eyes around the inaugural meeting of the Preston Volunteers, was moved to remark the 'total absence of the working-class element'. It has been suggested that the volunteer movement was an expression of a growing middle class in Victorian society, whose aspirations had palpably not been satisfied by the regular army, but there were also practical reasons why the working classes were in a minority. First and foremost was the expense of being a volunteer; without help the lower classes could not even buy a rifle and uniform.

Many units therefore tried to spread the costs of membership more fairly by having a subscription system; higher for officers and lower for other ranks. In the case of Bury, officers paid five guineas and the men one guinea. One of the cheapest corps to belong to was the Liverpool Welsh, which had an entrance fee of 10s. 6d. with uniforms being paid for by half-crown instalments. Bury lowered its 'other ranks' subscription to 10s. in 1861, and Rossendale similarly introduced a uniform-by-instalments system at sixpence a week, and this was seen explicitly as an inducement 'to the working classes'. Warrington also tried to encourage working men, but small sums were still a considerable barrier to the lowest in society and even the least pretentious units bulked large with skilled craftsmen, hotel keepers and specialist retailers. The composition of individual units is instructive; in 1862, for example, the 40th (Manchester) LRV numbered 77 who could be termed 'gentlemen' or professionals, 129 tradesmen, 82 clerks, 347 artisans from the foundries, and only 21 'labourers'.

The 39th (Liverpool Welsh) similarly had many clerks and book-keepers and the 80th (Liverpool 'Press Guard') were drawn mainly from the staffs of the *Albion, Mercury* and *Weekly Chronicle* newspapers. One should be careful, however, about making too sweeping a generalisation about the genteel nature of the movement, as there were certainly exceptions to the general rule. The 25th (Liverpool) were drawn mainly from the Mersey ironworks, and the 37th (Hawkshead) LRV were met wherever they went with the cry of 'Here comes t'Haakset Bootwangs', as their ranks contained so many cobblers. At Haigh the 26th LRV were mainly drawn mainly from colliery workers. It is also true that, as time progressed and the first flush of enthusiasm faded, the units became more working class and the average recruit younger. This was made possible by greater government support and involvement.

To get more recruits, buy equipment and encourage the less wealthy, many units adopted money-raising schemes like public subscriptions, or enrolling those who had no intention of turning up to drill and using their contributions to subsidise others. Some companies helped to impose discipline by a system of fines, the proceeds being spent for the good of the whole. Failure to attend compulsory drill in the Bolton LRV would cost 5s.,

Sergeant Bradshaw of the 62nd (Clitheroe) L.R.V. pictured c. 1880. Bradshaw finally served for a total of thirty-five years. (Clitheroe Museum.)

whilst the same in the Liverpool Scottish would result in a 2s. 6d. fine. The Scots also had fines for other offences; loading or shooting out of turn would cost half a crown but pointing a rifle, loaded or not, at another person without orders so to do carried a penalty of £1. Expulsion could be the result of the second offence.

Although the uniforms and drills of the volunteers could be the subject of mockery, the movement as a whole was often perceived as having an improving effect upon the community and a moral benefit to the individual. One Liverpool magistrate remarked,

> I have observed that many young men who before were lounging and idling, and spending their evenings in questionable places of amusement, are now quite changed. They come to drill and induce others to come, and the effect has been of a very beneficial character to the neighbourhood.

Average length of service in the rifle volunteers was only about four years, but there was a significant number who stayed for a good deal longer in the

LRV and its successor organisations. One such was Sergeant Bradshaw of the 62nd (Clitheroe) LRV who finally served a remarkable thirty-five years. Three members of the Hawkshead Company did twenty-one years or more continuous service each, and in 1884 one Manchester unit was able to state that it had 118 members who had served for ten years or more.

Weapons and Uniforms

BY THE MIDDLE OF THE NINETEENTH CENTURY European armies were changing from smooth-bored muskets to 'rifled' weapons. In the rifle, grooves cut inside the barrel spun the bullet, stabilising it in flight and leading to greater accuracy over longer ranges. When the volunteers were formed it was therefore natural that they should be 'rifle volunteers', and it was specified that their weapons should be of .577-inch calibre so as to be capable of using the same ammunition as the regulars. Most were equipped with the Pattern 1853 Enfield muzzle-loading rifled musket but other types were not unknown, especially for target and competition shooting. Lord Elcho, a renowned rifle enthusiast, advised volunteers to get Whitworth or Westley Richards breech-loaders if they could afford them, as they were most accurate at long ranges.

The Enfield itself was no mean weapon, not particularly fast to load but as accurate and reliable as anything used by foreign armies at the time of its introduction. One Yorkshire volunteer claimed to have shot a rabbit with one at one thousand yards. Technically the P53 was a single-shot percussion model; that is, it was set off by a percussion cap struck by a hammer. The small primary explosion of the cap set off the main charge and fired the bullet. The Enfield was designed as a successor to the 'Minie' rifle, a similar model which proved itself in the Crimea. The Enfield came in two lengths – a short type with two barrel bands holding the barrel to the fore end, and a long 'three-band' version. Generally the 'long' version was issued first, with many units later using the 'short'. According to one volunteer quoted in the *Manchester Guardian*,

> A first class regulation Enfield rifle and bayonet of Birmingham manufacture, may be had wholesale for £2 10s. I have purchased one through a friend – maker Daniel Leonard – at that price, and as sweet a piece was ever laid to shoulder. Allow me also to remark that with proper grease for the patch

The .577-inch Snider–Enfield breech-loading rifle. This privately-purchased example bears the inscription 'Presented to Capt. W. J. Stewart by the members of the 1st Lancashire College Cadets, Octr. 19th 1867.' (County Museum, Preston.)

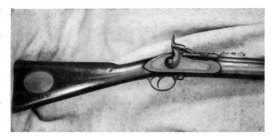

no fouling takes place, and that leading up of the barrel so much complained of in India, is caused by the peculiar composition in the manufacture of the cartridges, which must stand the heat of that climate.

In the mid-1860s the Enfield was beginning to show its age against recently evolved French and Prussian breech-loading models. Developing a completely new rifle would be a very expensive undertaking, so the existing weapons were modified. A hinged trap was inserted in the breech of the rifle allowing the use of fixed charge 'boxer' cartridges. This 'Snider' conversion turned the old muzzle-loading Enfield into a breech-loader and was a useful stopgap until a new arm could be issued. As late as 1878 regulations specified other ranks' arms in the volunteers as a 'Snider' rifle with ordinary bayonet whilst sergeants were to be equipped with a short 'Snider' with a 'sword' bayonet, also a brass-hilted sword.

The new Martini–Henry .45-inch calibre breech-loader entered service with the regular army in the early 1870s, being first manufactured in 1871 and taken up by the troops from 1874 onwards. Volunteers first received them officially in 1879, but photographic evidence suggests that many were purchased privately prior to this date.

By 1885 all volunteers had this weapon. It is now best known as the rifle used by British troops in the Zulu wars. It is interesting to note that, although originally volunteers had been expected to provide their own weapons, pressure from Lord Elcho and others soon influenced the government to begin issuing weapons at public expense. On 1 July 1859 the new Palmerston administration announced that it would issue twenty-five government weapons for every one hundred volunteers. At about the same time a manual entitled *Drill and Rifle Instruction for Volunteer Rifle Corps* was recommended. Eventually all rifles would be issued by the government and the drill would be uniform with the regulars.

Volunteers were also equipped with bayonets, of which there were two major types: the 'socket' bayonet, triangular in section, and the 'yataghan' sword

Ensign John Milligan, 71st (Liverpool Highland) L.R.V., pictured in 1862 in the kilted uniform of the corps, complete with highland basket-hilted broadsword. (Liverpool Scottish Museum.)

bayonet with a 22-inch blade, often used with the short rifle. Rifle units referred to their bayonets as 'swords' for they were traditionally longer than those issued with older patterns of musket in the line infantry. Bayonet drill was often practised, either with the standard manual or adaptations such as the *Panorama of the Volunteer Rifleman's Experience* published in 1860. It is surprising to relate that at least one volunteer bayonet saw use in anger; a lady of Satterthwaite, frightened by an intruder, grabbed one which belonged to a male relative and saw the interloper off the premises.

Volunteer weapons which belonged to a unit were usually marked and numbered. Ulverston, for example, paid £1 to have its sixty rifles numbered by a local craftsman. Privately-owned arms would not normally be marked but were often of better quality; also a number of presentation pieces still survive bearing suitable inscriptions. In 1878 regulations went into great detail on the care, storage and marking of the volunteers' arms. Weapons of the Lancashire Rifle Volunteers were now to bear a 'V' followed by the letters 'LCS', the number of the corps, and the number of the weapon within the unit. Sergeant instructors were required to keep detailed records of the rifles, their condition and spare parts available. Between uses the guns were to be kept in an approved armoury unless the volunteer had the written permission of his commanding officer to keep his rifle at home.

Whilst there was a fair degree of uniformity in arms, a good deal of latitude was allowed in the provision of uniform, approval for which could be granted at county level by the lord lieutenant. The result was a wide variety of dress, dependent mainly on the sartorial taste of the commanding officer and the wealth of the unit. The commonest coat colour was grey, but green, scarlet and blue were also found. The general assumption was that the

Left: Members of the 80th (Liverpool) 'Press Guard', L.R.V. by R. Simkin, 1879: left to right are an officer in full dress; an officer in undress wearing the dark blue frock coat and peacked forage cap with guards-style grenade badge; and a private soldier with the .45-inch Martini–Henry rifle and socket bayonet. (Board of Trustees of the National Museums and Galleries on Merseyside [King's Regimental Collection].)
Right: Captain J. L. Wood, 80th (Liverpool) 'Press Guard', L.R.V., c. 1880.
(Courtesy of Mr D. Reeves.)

volunteers would be employed as light infantry or skirmishers, and clothing usually reflected this role.

General Peel, secretary of state for war, had a committee produce a 'pattern' for uniform, but even so the early days of the movement were marked by dazzling variety. If anything approximated to a 'standard' uniform, it was that of the 27th (Bolton) LRV who chose a light grey tunic similar to that already adopted by Bury and Manchester, 'the skirt to be 16 inches in length with bronze mountings. Trousers of the same colour, shade and cloth as the tunic'. The facings of the coat were green. Three years later the 27th changed to scarlet jackets.

More adventurous were the 71st (Liverpool Highland), who were quick to adopt the kilt, and the Liverpool Press Guard (which one satirist dubbed the 'Press Gang Guard'), who began with Garibaldi-style red shirts which were soon swopped for uniforms in the style of the full dress of the

Lieutenant Colonel J. Hutchinson and officers of the 8th (Bury) L.R.V., 1872. The accoutrements worn include shakos with ball tufts, bands of lace being added for senior officers, and the 1827-pattern rifle officer's sword. The uniform was grey with black facings; scarlet was not adopted until the end of the decade.
(Lancashire Fusiliers Museum, Bury.)

footguards! Other units mimicked the green uniform of the King's Royal Rifle Corps. In Bury, democracy had been carried so far in the unit that four sample uniforms with different facing colours were made up and the result voted upon. The decision was for black facings and bright buttons to the grey uniform. These costumes were made up by Whiteside's of Manchester and Whitehead's of Bury at a cost of a little over 30s. each. This was quite a lot by the standards of the day, but most were more expensive than this, and the average cost of a uniform has been reckoned at £4 13s. 6d. Added to this would be the rifle and bayonet, belts and a greatcoat, to bring the total cost to over £10. A dock porter on the Mersey then earned 3s. 6d. per day.

One of the most expressive and expensive pieces of uniform was the head-gear. Most units wore a low shako, but even this could vary in many details including plume, tuft, peak shape, piping and materials; an officer's example could well cost 20s., and over half this for 'other ranks'. In at least one unit, the 6th (Manchester) LRV, the shako was quilted. Soft peaked forage caps were also worn, often as a form of 'undress' headwear. Busbies were not unknown, and among those surviving is an excellent example worn by the officers of the 76th (Farnworth) LRV in the 1870s. The Liverpool Press Guard or 80th (Liverpool) LRV hoped to outdo all others by adopting the guard's bearskin, but the ultimate idiosyncrasy was that of Captain W. T. Johnson, adjutant of the 5th (Liverpool) LRV. He had once belonged to a unit of irregular light horse in the Indian army, and on special occasions appeared in its dress uniform complete with multi-coloured turban.

It was hardly surprising that the most outlandish volunteer uniforms attracted a good deal of ribaldry. Hugh Shimmin, writing in the Liverpool *Porcupine* of 8 December 1860, described the volunteers as 'Pseudo Warriors' who 'morning noon and night strut about in military attire. The uniform, and not the cause is their attraction . . . and the promenade, the ballrooms, the theatre are all invaded by these over-dressed foplings, even the sanctuary of the church is set at naught'.

The Wigan men were also the victims of many witticisms. Their

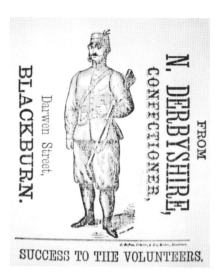

Depiction of a soldier of the 2nd (Blackburn) L.R.V. from a paper bag, c. 1870. (Lancashire County Library.)

uniforms, which had been ordered from Edwards of London, began to arrive in January 1860. These were dark grey with red facings and bronze buttons bearing the inscription 'WVR' and the rose, their caps were covered with an oilskin cover in bad weather and a green and black feather plume for ceremonial. Other accoutrements were of patent leather, and regular-army-style gaiters were worn. Though this was hardly flamboyant by the standards of the time, it was suggested that they resembled 'Woolwich Convicts' or the inmates of a workhouse 'taking an airing', or even that, when marching they could be mistaken for a funeral procession. Many of the company were heavy pipe-smokers and so the local wits put it about that this was a new military tactic, advances being made under cover of the smog.

Certainly not all Lancashire volunteers were dandified; the most sober units clad in grey uniforms were strongly reminiscent of the Confederate forces in the American Civil War, and this was not entirely fortuitous. After all, grey was also the colour of the American reserve forces and many supplies for the South came from England. Neither is this a recent observation, for the Marquis of Hartington remarked upon it at the time. The marquis himself excited comment in Berlin in 1866 where he appeared at the Prussian victory parade celebrating the defeat of Austria in his volunteer uniform, much to the mystification of the 'junkers'.

Lord Elcho was one of the leading advocates of simplicity in attire. Writing to Thomas Fairbairn of Manchester in November 1859 he recommended,

> Be economical in dress, and what you save in braid and needless ornament, spend in instructors and the best arms you can obtain. Now, my experience at Hythe [school of musketry] has shown me that a volunteer may neatly, comfortably and efficiently be clothed for 28s., that is cap, blouse and peg top trousers, to which must be added 8s. or 10s. for belt and pouch. This was the cost of my Hythe equipment, of which the 'Times' expressed a favourable opinion. The material was a grey woollen serge, strong and wiry . . . the blouse being loose, is as easy as a shirt.

He went on to suggest that leggings be worn with the trousers and that the whole ensemble be grey with a view to camouflage, 'the dark green and pepper and salt uniforms being at a distance, more distinct and visible than red'.

In his opinion a good greatcoat was more desirable than any amount of foppery. His remarks were supported by General Sir William Napier, who observed that, in battle between a volunteer rifle corps and regular troops, the outcome would depend largely 'upon the former's skill in hiding'. Subdued and practical dress was therefore necessary.

The authorities would also have liked to make the uniforms more restrained, and at various times the War Office did issue directives that the lord lieutenant should only approve styles for new units which matched those already in existence in the county. However, in Lancashire and many other places this was a losing battle, because approval for a uniform could not be withdrawn once given, and many different styles were already in being. Details were also sniped at, perhaps more successfully; volunteer officers were forbidden gold braid, which was reserved for the regulars, and attempts were made to restrict the carrying of swords to commissioned officers and sergeants on duty or travelling to their duty. Even so, things like button design and facing colours were to remain entirely the prerogative of the corps throughout most of the period in question.

At the outset rifle volunteer units were not permitted to carry the officially-sanctioned, consecrated and much-revered flags which in the regulars were known as 'colours'. This was not perhaps surprising, as the volunteers were intended to be auxiliaries whose main role would be skirmishing. It may have been this which prompted local dignitaries to give other items to volunteer units. A particularly favourite presentation piece was a bugle, usually suitably inscribed and understood to be the symbol of light and skirmishing troops. The Salford companies received no fewer than four such bugles in 1860.

Nonetheless, many Lancashire rifle volunteer units did carry unofficial 'flags' which the authorities would not have recognised to be 'colours' in the true sense. No comprehensive survey has been conducted, but the early 1860s furnish three good examples of the practice. A 'beautiful banner' was presented by J. R. Wolfendon, the mayor of Bolton, to the town's rifle volunteers in 1862. It was described as 'green silk with the crown and bugle and XXVII, LRV, A.D. MDCCCLXII in the centre and surrounded by a yellow border upon which was displayed at intervals the Lancashire Rose'.

Silver presentation bugles, both dated 1860. The one with the cord attached was given by 'a few of the ladies of Preston' to the 11th (Preston) L.R.V., the other by Eleanor Cecily Clifton to the 29th (Lytham) L.R.V. (County Museum, Preston.)

In May the same year the 9th (Warrington) LRV received two flags which the local newspaper described as a 'Queen's Colour' and a 'Regimental Colour', both bearing the legend 'The Ninth Lancashire Rifle Corps', with the latter also emblazoned with the borough arms and the motto 'Efficienta'. At about the same time the 2nd (Blackburn) also had one or more flags which were suspiciously like colours in their configuration. One appears in the painting by Wladimir Sherwood of the laying of the foundation stone of the Blackburn Exchange on 10 March 1863, which now hangs in Blackburn Museum.

Perhaps the strangest flag presentation of all was that of the 5th (Press Company) of the 40th (Manchester) LRV in 1859. In this case the colours of the Manchester and Salford Volunteers of 1803 were disinterred and re-presented to the new unit. Whether the half-century-old colours were actually carried by the company and whether they were regarded as official is not recorded.

Later volunteer battalions, excepting those who retained rifle dress, were officially permitted colours, but this was still at their own expense. Territorial colours were not purchased with public funds until after the Second World War. The general trend appears to have been an increasing similarity to regular colours so that, eventually, the only significant difference was the battalion number, usually displayed as a roman numeral in the top left-hand corner.

Bands

IN THE REGULAR ARMY it was usual for each regiment to have a band. In time of war the bandsmen could serve as stretcher-bearers; drums in the line and bugles in the light infantry and rifles could also give elementary musical signals to the fighting troops. If anything, the number of musicians was larger in the rifle volunteers than the regulars, for in 1860 it was often the case that even company-sized units aspired to have a band. Sometimes rifle volunteer units signed contracts with existing civilian bands, but this could prove expensive as they were not yet regarded as a necessary expense by the War Office.

Some settled for fifes and drums, but in Lancashire brass bands were already popular and some members of works bands were also volunteer bandsmen. One of the best known bands was the Bacup band, which played with the 4th (Rossendale) LRV. This was established in 1859 under the leadership of John Stevenson; it normally had twenty-three players, and between 1862 and its dissolution in 1871 it won prizes in forty-eight contests, thirty-two of these being first places. The total prize money taken was £1,370 5s., plus instruments to the value of £300.

Occasionally the volunteers faced the problem of having simply too many bands. At Knowsley in 1860 special instructions had to be issued that only the regimental (battalion) bands would play at the march-past, while all the extra bands walked along behind their brigades. At one volunteer drill in the Lake District, no fewer than five bands attended, all playing at once. A spectator described the resulting noise as 'somewhat overwhelming'.

Bandsmen often had special uniforms finer than those of the rank and file, and sometimes the regular infantry practice was followed of using the facing colour of the soldiers' collars and cuffs for the colour of the bandsmen's coats. Again, like the regulars, volunteer bandsmen were frequently issued with a short decorative sword to hang at the waist. Some were especially fine, with a plethora of decoration and engraving, but others followed the line pattern of 1856 with its relatively simple hilt of cast brass or white metal.

Detailed regulations concerning band establishments were laid down in 1881. These allowed the recruitment as musicians of boys between the ages of twelve and seventeen, up to two per company as drummers and buglers, and twelve in the band, in addition to adults. On camp, no more than twelve bandsmen were to be allowed for each corps.

The band of the 2nd (Blackburn) L.R.V. at Cleveleys, 1868. The drum major with his staff, and a very young drummer are to the left of the group.
(Queen's Lancashire Regiment Collection.)

Bandsman's sword, 31st (Oldham) L.R.V., c. 1860. This essentially ornamental short sword is based on the regular 'Sword, Drummer's, Mark I' of 1856. (County Museum, Preston.)

Drum Major James Sivell, 6th (Manchester) L.R.V., c. 1875. The Drum Major wears his four rank chevrons low on the sleeve in the fashion general between about 1870 and 1881. The medals were awarded for regular service in India and the Middle East with the 14th Light Dragoons. (14th/20th King's Hussars Collection, County Museum, Preston.)

Reorganisation and Reviews

BY THE SUMMER OF 1860, Lancashire Rifle Volunteers were well enough equipped for several major reviews. A national review by the queen and prince consort saw twenty thousand volunteers from all over the country march past in Hyde Park. The first significant local inspection was that of the Lancashire and Cheshire volunteers held at Chester on 20 June 1860, and this was followed by Warrington Field Day on 6 August, which included not only the 9th (Warrington) LRV but units from Liverpool, Newton-le-Willows, St Helens and Cheshire. Only five days later came the 'Grand Review' at Newton-le-Willows, where the total number of troops on parade topped eight thousand, including not only rifle volunteers but mounted volunteers from the Lancashire Hussars and the Duke of Lancaster's Own Yeomanry. Even this paled into insignificance beside the review held at Knowsley Park on 1 September 1860. Here, over twelve thousand Lancashire volunteers were present, including four brigades of rifles, volunteer artillery, the Lancashire Hussars and the mounted rifle volunteers.

At Knowsley each volunteer rifle company was allocated its own tent, amply supplied, by courtesy of the Earl of Derby, with 'refreshments for sixty men, one beer can containing three gallons of ale and ten half pint drinking cups'. More beer, twenty-five hogsheads in all and brewed at Knowsley, was available so that the cans could be refilled until every man had had his pint. There was also lemonade to drink, and no less than five tons of pies, in the making of which 8,000 lbs of flour, 6,000 lbs of veal and ham, 500 lbs of butter and 2,000 eggs had been used.

The Knowsley Review was generally a great success, but there were a few who were disappointed. The newly raised 75th (Broughton) LRV wished to attend and had uniforms, but found that, in the limited time available, their drill could not be made sufficiently accomplished for them to march. The 37th (Ulverston) did go but, being short of numbers for the band, co-opted three schoolboys. These were unceremoniously dumped off the train at Cark by an officer because they were not in uniform. The bandmaster felt it his duty to remain with them, and he resigned soon after.

Despite minor mishaps of this nature, the review at Knowsley had clearly made a great impact on press and public alike. One observer of the parade, Christopher North, remarked,

Melancholy indeed to think that all these fine, fierce, ferocious fire-eaters are doomed, but for some unlooked-for revolution in the affairs of Europe and the World, to die in their beds.

North was substantially correct, but some of Lancashire's volunteers did make efforts to perish on the field of honour. Some men of the 1st (Liverpool) LRV had served with Garibaldi's British Legion in 1859, and their commander later received, in recognition of his service, a photograph of the great man signed from 'a Soldier of Liberty to Soldiers of Liberty' – though, strictly speaking, all this was contrary to the Foreign Enlistment Act. Salford volunteers were called out 'in aid of the Civil Power' in 1867, and in 1878 the 17th (Burnley) LRV offered themselves to serve in the Mediterranean, but were not required.

In terms of ceremony one of the most unexpected coups of the period was achieved by the 10th (Lancaster) LRV on 15 October 1860. On that day Queen Victoria stopped to have lunch at the station and the unit formed part of the honour guard resplendent in their new grey uniforms with scarlet facings and 'Glengarry' caps.

The total number of volunteers in the United Kingdom now exceeded 150,000; more men than the regular army. That this huge body had little organisation above company level was clearly ridiculous, but higher organisation required government intervention and, ultimately, public money. In January 1860 the first inspector general of volunteers was appointed, and on 24 March the War Office had allowed the making of 'consolidated battalions' whereby several companies from the 'same town or city' would make up one larger unit. Later in the year 'administrative battalions' were authorised, drawing in companies from wide areas not yet 'consolidated' to make up new battalions. Ex-regular officers could now be appointed to the battalions as adjutants and took care of administration and training. These were funded at first by the units, but later were the responsibility of the army, and received pay.

Re-organisation took some time, and occasionally companies were moved from one battalion to another. Taking the Blackburn area as an example, corps in this locality came under the 8th Administrative Battalion; this naturally included the 2nd Corps which had been formed in the town in 1859, and the 3rd Corps which the 2nd had already absorbed. Also attached were the 62nd (Clitheroe) and the 81st (Withnell) Corps.

In all, nine Lancashire administrative battalions were formed. Two of these were based in Liverpool and the rest at Burnley, Eccles, Ulverston, Preston, Ashton-under-Lyne, Blackburn and Warrington. It was now possible for the volunteers to begin to develop a command structure above that at company level. In Liverpool in May 1861, for instance, Nathaniel Bousfield, rather than simply being the captain of the 1st Liverpool Company of the LRV, was now lieutenant-colonel of a whole battalion. Under him was a major in the shape of James B. Taylor, an adjutant, a surgeon, and an honorary chaplain. The 1st, 22nd, 38th, 45th, 66th and 69th LRV who made up the battalion included no fewer than nine captains, nine lieutenants and eight ensigns.

It was also during the early 1860s that pressure increased for public money to be spent on the volunteers; few communities were going to be able to raise gifts and subscriptions every year, as they had done in 1859 and 1860, and higher degrees of organisation meant greater expense. In 1863 it was agreed to subsidise the movement from government funds to the tune of £1 *per annum* per man, a figure later increased to £1 10s. Interestingly, volunteer officers' commissions, like regular commissions, became marketable property and were sometimes bought and sold, for as much as £100 or as little as £3 depending on rank and battalion.

At the same time economic depression and the 'cotton famine' associated with the American Civil War made less private money available, and the overall effect was a gradual change in the social composition of volunteer units. A good number of working men, previously barred by their inability to pay for uniform, were now able to join due to the availability of public funds, whilst some middle-class men, their willingness to participate ebbing as they saw the danger of invasion recede, went on to pastures new.

Better organisation made more demanding and realistic forms of training possible. In 1862 manoeuvres were held representing attacks on Liverpool, the Liverpudlians defending their own city against the attackers, many of whom were Mancunians; one of the brigades deployed at Altcar was made up of the 1st, 2nd and 3rd Manchesters, together with the Ardwick Corps.

Also in 1862, and coinciding with the Guild celebrations, was the 'Great Volunteer Review and sham fight' on Preston Moor. About 3,200 volunteers took part, watched by a crowd estimated at 30,000 people. The reviewing officer was Major-General Scarlett, who had led the Charge of the Heavy Brigade at Balaklava. After taking the salute, he

> passed along the whole line, which extended over near a mile in length and minutely inspected the troops each Corps striking up a march on his reaching its right, and continuing until his arrival at the next.

The volunteers then marched past, receiving cheers as they passed the saluting point and grandstand which were situated at a point about midway between the Lancaster–Preston highway and Deepdale Road. Prominent in the column were the Preston, Bolton, Blackburn and St Helens Corps, and the youths of Rossall College who had 'received a flattering reception as, of course, was most proper from the ladies'.

Mock battle followed, with skirmishing and artillery fire as well as crashing volleys from the companies. The overall effect was spoilt only by the collapse of one of the stands nearest to Garstang Road, which 'gave way without a moment's warning, and the scores that congregated upon it precipitated to the ground'. There were no fatalities, but several were injured and, as the *Fleetwood Chronicle* reported, 'great excitement ensued'.

In 1866 many Lancashire men attended the review of the northern volunteers at York, where the total number of volunteer troops present was over twenty thousand. There was another big review at Sefton Park in 1867, and many smaller events over the next few years. In 1871 there was a sham fight and review at Heaton Park, and Manchester Rifle Volunteers also took part in a similar action at Somerford Park in Cheshire. In 1875 the Manchester LRV took on Bury at Prestwich in an outpost skirmish, an action which was marred by heavy rain.

Camps

ONE OF THE MOST INTERESTING aspects of reviews and realistic training sessions, which might involve travel to distant ranges, was the evolution of the idea of the camp. To start with these were very *ad hoc* affairs often organised, and sometimes funded, by company officers. By 1880 they were to be officially sanctioned, paid for, and even expected, both by the general officer commanding the district and by the War Office. Bolton LRV was said to be one of the first to hold regular 'encampments' and, indeed, made summer pilgrimages to Lytham for this purpose for over a decade from 1867, changing to Rhyl when financial arrangements altered and 'the well known attractions of Lytham had somewhat paled'. Bolton may have claims to being one of the first to make regular camps at the same venue, but the idea of spending time away to train was as old as the volunteer movement itself, especially when a unit had limited range facilities at home. Indeed, Nathaniel Bousfield had taken his Liverpool contingent under canvas at Crosby as early as 1860.

Lieutenant Henry Mann, 8th (Bury) L.R.V. by his bell tent on camp at Fleetwood, c.
1876. Visible within the tent are his trunk, camp bed, table and wash bowl. Other ranks
had far less luxurious accommodation, eight to a tent; regulations would later specify
three officers per tent, or twelve other ranks!
(Lancashire Fusiliers Museum, Bury.

One Lancashire officer who did more for the idea of the camp than most was
Major, subsequently Lieutenant-Colonel, Mellor of the 8th (Bury) LRV. Tiring
of the bell tents and damp marquees which they had occupied at Fleetwood
each year from 1872 to 1879, he was instrumental in moving the camp to
Pensarn in Wales. Here the officers found ready for their reception

> A most comfortable, and by comparison luxurious, hut, the walls and roof
> of timber all bolted together in sections so as to be easily portable, lighted
> by 16 windows by day and by duplex lamps at night; the floor carpeted,
> and to crown all a bright fire in a handsome stove.

Furthermore, both this mess hut and a similar one provided for the sergeants
were turned to financial advantage. They were hired out to other corps and
finally, when the camp venue was moved from Conway to Lytham, they
were sold.

At Lytham the Bury men now established a remarkable camp in a
forty-acre field. At one end of this were eighty bell tents for the men, plus
twenty-four officers' tents, quartermaster's stores and guard tents, the whole
camp being arranged in eight lines. Each of the other ranks' bell tents was

occupied by eight men, each man having a palliasse, two blankets, water-proof pillow and sheet. The officers, by contrast, had iron bedsteads, washstands, a compact chest of drawers and a small table. The 'mess tent' was, in fact, a semi-permanent structure with a felt roof, the walls 'draped with flowered calico' and the windows hung with lace curtains!

In several instances a regular camp seems to have sprung directly from the need for a suitable range. This was certainly the case with Altcar, but it also played a part in the selection of other coastal sites; not only Crosby, Lytham, Fleetwood and the Welsh locations previously noted, but also Southport, Grange, Carnforth, St Annes, Cleveleys and Blackpool. Sometimes locations had been pioneered by the yeomanry and militia, a circumstance which would have helped the volunteer camps gain acceptance from the local populace.

On the Ranges

DEFINITE IMPROVEMENT was made in skill at arms during the 1860s. There were local ranges for practice, but there was also a national rifle competition held at Wimbledon, and volunteers were able to win and wear badges for proficiency with the rifle. Some photographs show marksmen festooned with shooting badges and medals, but only two types were universal: one of these was the crossed muskets of the 'sergeant instructor in musketry'; the other was a series of four graded badges introduced in 1861 showing, respectively, an unadorned rifle, a rifle with one star, with two stars and with three stars. As originally sanctioned, these denoted the best shots in the unit at 300 yards, from 350 to 600 yards, and marksmen obtaining specified points at 900 yards.

The 1881 regulations allowed for no other type of badge for 'class' shooting, but did allow 'authorised prize shooting badges to be worn on the arm'. Many volunteers were already taking full advantage of this, and the best shots sometimes had their entire left sleeve covered in gaudy patches. Some also wore shooting medals on the right breast, which was technically an infringement of regulations because the only medals sanctioned for wear here were those for saving human life.

The Altcar ground was undoubtedly the best known of the Lancashire rifle ranges, and it continues in territorial army use to this day. Originally Liverpool Rifle Volunteers had shot on the shore at Dingle and Crosby

The 65th (Rossall) L.R.V. on an 800-yard range, from a French print c.1870. The uniform of the Rossall Corps was changed from grey to scarlet c.1863. The intimate connection between the school and the volunteers is emphasised by the presence of a master. (Rossall School Archive.)

against improvised calico targets, or inside an old ship-building shed, but two officers of the Liverpool LRV, Adam A. Gladstone and Robert J. Tinley, approached the Earl of Sefton for the lease of land at a place then known as Ballings Wharf. Despite the fact that Alt Grange was already let, the existing tenant, a Mr Robert Clarke, proved most co-operative. On Saturday 28 July 1860 the first round was fired by the Earl of Sefton himself, using an Enfield rifle. Soon thirty firing points and targets were available and the site became generally known as Hightown range.

On 29 October 1860 the 'Grand Lancashire Rifle' contest was held. Shooting continued for a week and special trains to the competition were laid on from Exchange Station, Liverpool. The impartial umpire was Colonel Clarke Kennedy, inspector of the Stirlingshire Militia. Rules of the competition were those generally pertaining to the National Rifle Association and many prizes, up to the then remarkable sum of one hundred guineas, were presented. An artillery volunteer band provided music, including the 'Hightown Rifle Contest Galop', specially composed by bandmaster G. A. Wielopolski Phillips. A similar contest was held at Barrow in 1862.

Though Altcar was the best known range, there were many others, of which at least three were in the Manchester area: Barton Moss, Heaton Park and Ancoats. This last was perhaps the least successful and most shortlived, being the private property of a rifle salesman who allowed his rifle volunteer customers to use it. Closure was precipitated when a neighbouring cottager put in a claim for smashed crockery.

Another range with an indifferent record was that at Roosecote used by volunteers from the Lake District. During a competition there in November

1861 a labourer was fatally wounded when Ulverston volunteers fired into a railway embankment, not realising there was anyone working there. In another incident in 1879 James Leadbetter, a rifle volunteer who was acting as shotmarker, was shot through the thigh by one of his comrades.

Fleetwood also had a range, and as early as October 1859 units travelled there for rifle instruction. One such was the 4th (Rossendale) LRV, whose visit was somewhat spoilt by bad weather 'very unfavourable to outdoor practice', the company being forced to drill instead in the North Euston Hotel. These early experiments may have set something of a precedent, for in the period 1860 to 1867 Fleetwood became home to a school of musketry which trained officers and NCOs of both the regular and volunteer forces. Sometimes the volunteers were able to shoot better than the regulars; this, the local *Chronicle* explained, was the result of the volunteers using their own weapons, and the element of self-selection which the voluntary force entailed.

Bolton LRV quickly obtained land for a shooting range of three hundred yards beside the river at Bradshaw. This was hired to them for £5 *per annum* by the public-spirited Mr Hardcastle, who used the money as a prize for the best shot. A longer range was obtained for them at Kersley Moss in 1861, but this had to be closed due to 'new works and buildings springing up in dangerous proximity'. Wigan's first ground, between Brock Mill and Jolly mill, was also less than ideally placed, again due to nearby buildings.

In the case of the 11th (Preston) LRV, expansion of the corps and expansion of the area required for shooting entailed several moves for the volunteer range. During 1859 and 1860 it was at Brockholes, within comfortable walking distance of the town centre. For the next five years the venue was Hutton Marsh, and finally land was acquired near Longridge which did good service both for practice and for annual prize competitions.

A parallel development to the rifle volunteer movement itself was the founding of a County Rifle Association for Lancashire, the inaugural meeting taking place in Preston on 28 December 1860. Lord Stanley was to be chairman of the new association, and John Blundell the secretary. Lancashire then formed a team to shoot in national matches at Wimbledon, beating Middlesex to win in 1862, and both Gloucestershire and Middlesex in 1863. Although the County Rifle Association and the rifle volunteers were separate bodies, the relationship was always close and members of one were often members of the other.

Individual shooting successes achieved by Lancashire Rifle Volunteers included two Queen's Prize wins; Private Jamieson, 15th (Liverpool) LRV in 1877, and Corporal Taylor, 47th (St Helens) LRV in 1879. There were also wins and placings in the Prince Consort's, the Prince of Wales'

Prize tankards. The larger commemorates the victory of the Lancashire Rifle Volunteers over Middlesex in the shooting competition of 1862 and carries the names of the ten team members who were drawn from the 5th, 8th, 13th, 26th, 40th and 70th Volunteers, and included Sergeant Duggan (or Dougan) of Haigh. The smaller tankard was awarded as a sports prize on 1 October 1860 by the 65th (Rossall) L.R.V. (County Museum, Preston.)

Private G. Jamieson, 15th (Liverpool) L.R.V., winner of the Queen's prize at Wimbledon in 1877. On his left arm are two shooting prize badges, in his hand the Martini–Henry rifle, complete with a metal fore sight guard. (Board of Trustees of the National Museums and Galleries on Merseyside.)

and other prizes. There would have been three clear wins in the Queen's Prize for Lancashire Rifle Volunteers but for the case of Corporal Peake of the Manchester LRV in 1868. He achieved the highest score but was disqualified for a breach of the rules. An enquiry later cleared him of any impropriety, but the judges' decision on the day was final, and the prize went to Lieutenant Carslake of the 5th (Bridgewater) Somerset Rifle Volunteers.

A particularly ingenious shot among Lancashire competitors was Sergeant Dougan of the 26th (Haigh) LRV. Though he never won a Queen's Prize, he did carry away two rifles and medals in Wimbledon contests. He even manufactured his own rifle, which weighed 14 lbs and was thus excluded from the proceedings. He had more success with his special sights, which were of a 'peep-hole' variety inspired by those in use in America.

Cardwell and Volunteer Battalions

F ROM 1870 BEGAN A SERIES OF REFORMS associated with secretary of state
Edward Cardwell. There were immediate financial and administrative
implications, including the order that volunteer commissions would all be
issued by the Crown, and not purchased, but the first organisational changes
which affected the rifle volunteers came in 1873. At that date the United
Kingdom was divided into seventy infantry sub-districts, within which two
line battalions and the militia and volunteers were grouped into a sub-district brigade. Five years later, and mainly as a financial expedient, Viscount
Bury's committee on the volunteer force recommended that all remaining
administrative battalions be consolidated. This was carried out during 1880
and the last of the separate small corps were dissolved into battalions,
becoming lettered companies of the larger body. Battalion drills at annual
camps were now a requirement.

In Lancashire several corps were especially affected by these changes:
the 8th (Blackburn) Administrative Battalion, which was re-numbered as
2nd Corps and took in the units at Darwen and Clitheroe; the 4th
(Burnley), which was re-numbered 3rd and took in the units at Padiham,
Accringtom, Haslingden, Ramsbottom, Stackshead and Lytham; the
'new' 4th (Manchester) Corps, which took in Wigan, Swinton, Eccles,
Leigh, Atherton, Worsley, Farnworth and Flixton; the 7th (Ashton-under-Lyne), which included Oldham; the 9th (Warrington), which had a
company at Newton-le-Willows; the 10th (Ulverston), which included all
the Furness units; and the 11th (Preston), which now included Leyland
and Chorley. By the end of 1880 the Lancashire Rifle Volunteers were
therefore reduced to twenty-one numbered corps with a twenty-second
formed at Oldham in 1882. The reforms also introduced certificates of
efficiency and month-long courses for officers, who would either attend
a school or be attached to a regular unit.

What Cardwell had begun was finished by Hugh Childers, the new
secretary of state for war. Not only were the paired regular battalions of the
army fused into one unit, but the rifle volunteers were now attached to them
as volunteer battalions of the regular regiments. One example will serve to
show how this worked in practice. Following the general policy of 1881, the
11th (Preston) Corps became in 1883 the 1st Volunteer Battalion, Loyal
North Lancashire Regiment. Its strength of 824 all ranks was actually
composed of three elements: the first five companies – A, B, C, D and E –

Officers of the 2nd (Blackburn) Corps at Cleveleys with their ladies, 1879. Notice the blue cloth 'home service' spiked helmets which were introduced about this time. Artillery volunteers were distinguished by a ball instead of a spike.
(Queen's Lancashire Regiment Collection.)

Captain R. W. Baynes, 9th (Warrington) Corps., c.1886. Baynes is wearing the undress forage cap with the Lancashire rose and numeral of his unit. The broad band of lace around the cap is of oak-leaf pattern. Such a hat would have cost about 16s. 6d. when new.
(South Lancashire Regiment Museum, Warrington.)

were from Preston and totalled 531 effectives; Leyland, which had been the 59th LRV, provided F Company consisting of 53 men; Chorley, once the 61st LRV, supplied the remaining 240 soldiers to make up G, H and J Companies.

The years 1878 and 1881 also saw the issue by the War Office of the new sets of 'Regulations for the Volunteer Force'. These covered in great detail such matters as establishments, instructors, stores, uniform and paperwork. On the subject of uniform colour these regulations noted that 'Application for permission to change the colour of the uniform of Rifle Volunteer Corps will be favourably considered, provided the change be to Scarlet'. Thus it was that the splendid but eccentric volunteer uniforms of the 1860s and early 1870s progressively gave way to red, and by 1889 sixteen of the Lancashire's twenty-two volunteer

The new 'orders of dress' issued for the 1st Volunteer Battalion, The King's Own Royal Lancaster Regiment, 1883. (King's Own Museum, Lancaster.)

battalions were in scarlet. The exceptions to the rule, who maintained rifle-style green uniforms, were the 1st, 2nd and 5th Volunteer Battalions of the King's Liverpool Regiment, the 2nd Volunteer Battalion of the South Lancashire Regiment, and the 1st and 5th Volunteer Battalions of the Manchester Regiment.

Badges were also changed to match the new parent units, those on the head-dresses being distinguishable from the regulars usually only by the words (or an abbreviation of the words) 'volunteer battalion', and a number. Where previously the corps and county had appeared on shoulder-straps, these were changed to a 'V' and the title of the parent unit. All volunteers were warned to be careful on all occasions to

> appear either in the authorised uniform of their Corps, or in purely civilian dress. The unsoldierlike appearance of volunteers dressed partly in

Officer and Senior NCOs of the 1st Volunteer Battalion The Lancashire Fusiliers, on a camp at Conway, 1890. The uniform is now almost indistinguishable from the regulars, with fusilier cap and scarlet tunic. Notice the 'crossed rifle' badge of the sergeant instructors of musketry, and the 'Austrian knots' on the volunteers' sleeves. Rank chevrons are worn on the right sleeve only, as in the regulars at this date. (Lancashire Fusiliers Museum, Bury.)

uniform, partly in civilian costume, brings discredit not only on themselves but on the Force to which they belong.

The change of uniform and style was not purely for the sake of standardisation, but underlined a fundamental change of thinking on the part of the authorities. When first formed, the volunteers had been intended as a host of skirmishers; good shots, but with only basic drill, who would harry an invading force. They would aid, but would not actually be directly linked to, the regular force. Twenty years later they were seen as acting as supplementary battalions to the regulars, performing much the same duties and dressed in much the same uniform. The volunteers were now truly accepted as a part of the army proper, and the basis of the system which was to bring into being the territorial force in 1908 was laid. What had begun as a colourful, disorganised wave of popular enthusiasm, was to end as one of the pillars of national defence.

Appendix I: The Lancashire Rifle Volunteers 1859–81

1st (Liverpool) formed 11 June 1859; 1st Admin. Bn 1863; part of 1st Corps.

2nd (Blackburn) formed 4 October 1859; 8th Admin. Bn 1864; consolidated 2nd Corps 1880.

3rd (Blackburn) merged with 2nd Blackburn 1860.

4th (Rossendale) formed 4 July 1859; 3rd Admin. Bn 1861; consolidated 3rd Corps 1880.

5th (Liverpool) formed 19 August 1859; 2nd Admin. Bn 1861; part of 5th Lancashire (The Liverpool Rifle Volunteer Brigade) from 1862.

6th (Manchester), sometimes known as 1st Manchester, formed 25 August 1859; became 6th Corps.

7th (Accrington) formed 20 September 1859; 3rd Admin. Bn 1861; consolidated 3rd Corps 1880.

8th (Bury) formed 22 August 1859; consolidated 2nd Corps 1880.

9th (Warrington) formed 16 September 1859; 9th Admin. Bn 1865; consolidated 9th Corps 1880.

10th (Lancaster) formed 20 September 1859; 5th Admin. Bn 1862; consolidated 10th Corps 1876.

11th (Preston) formed 4 October 1859; 6th Admin. Bn 1861; consolidated 11th Corps 1880.

12th (Preston) formed 7 October 1859; merged with 11th (Preston).

13th (Southport) formed October 1859; attached to 1st (Liverpool) 1863; transferred to 15th Corps 1873.

14th (Edge Hill) formed 10 November 1859; 2nd Admin. Bn 1861; merged with 1st (Liverpool) 1862.

15th (Liverpool) formed 10 January 1860; 15th Corps.

16th not formed.

17th (Burnley) formed 16 January 1860; 3rd Admin. Bn 1860; consolidated 3rd Corps 1880.

18th not formed.

19th (Liverpool Scottish) formed 18 January 1860; 2nd Admin. Bn 1860; part of 5th Lancashire (The Liverpool Rifle Volunteer Brigade).

20th not formed.

21st (Wigan) formed 20 January 1860; 4th Admin. Bn 1869; consolidated 4th Corps 1880.

22nd (Liverpool) formed 30 January 1860; 1st Admin. Bn 1860; disbanded 1863.

23rd (Ashton-under-Lyne) formed 7 February 1860; 7th Admin. Bn 1863; consolidated 7th Corps 1880.

24th (Rochdale) formed 24 February 1860; redesignated 12th Corps 1880.

25th (Liverpool) formed 9 January 1860; absorbed into 8th Lancashire Artillery Volunteers in 1864.

26th (Haigh) formed 9 February 1860; disbanded 1864.

27th (Bolton) formed 2 December 1859 but only received this number in 1860 when it reached company strength; amalgamated with 82nd (Hindley) 1876; re-numbered 14th Corps 1880.

28th (Manchester) formed 21 February 1860; absorbed 70th (Droylesden) 1860 and was itself absorbed by 33rd (Ardwick) 1864.

29th (Lytham) formed 28 January 1860; 3rd Admin. Bn 1864; consolidated 3rd Corps 1880.

30th (Fishwick) formed 16 January 1860; absorbed into 11th (Preston) 1860.

31st (Oldham) formed 1 February 1860; 7th Admin. Bn 1863; consolidated 7th Corps 1880; formed 22nd Corps 1882.

32nd (Liverpool) formed 28 January 1860, sometimes known as Victoria Rifles; 2nd Admin. Bn 1862; absorbed by 5th Lancashire (The Liverpool Rifle Volunteer Brigade).

33rd (Ardwick) formed 28 January 1860; absorbed the 28th (Manchester) 1863; became 20th Corps 1880.

34th not formed.

35th not formed.

36th (Accrington) formed 7 January 1860; absorbed by 7th (Accrington) 1861.

37th (Ulverston) formed 29 February 1860, sometimes known as North Lonsdale; 1861 subdivided into five parts: 37A (Ulverston); 37B (Barrow); 37C (Hawkshead); 52nd (Dalton); and 53rd (Cartmel), all 5th Admin. Bn; consolidated 10th Corps 1876.

38th (Fairfield) originally formed 20 January 1860 but not numbered 38th until a few months later; 1st Admin. Bn May 1860; part of 1st Corps.

39th (Liverpool) formed 2 February 1860, sometimes called the Liverpool Welsh; 2nd Admin. Bn May 1860; part of 5th Lancashire (The Liverpool Rifle Volunteer Brigade) from 1862.

40th (Manchester) formed 16 February 1860; disbanded 1864.

42nd (Childwall) formed 3 March 1860; part of 5th Lancashire (The Liverpool Rifle Volunteer Brigade) 1864; disappears from Army Lists 1870.

43rd (Fallowfield) formed 11 February 1860; merged with 6th (Manchester) 1861.

44th (Longton) formed 2 March 1860; absorbed into 11th (Preston) 1866.

45th (Liverpool) formed 27 February 1860; 1st Admin. Bn 1860; part of 1st Corps.

46th (Swinton) formed 24 February 1860 and absorbed into 6th (Manchester) in October.

47th (St Helens) formed 29 February 1860; amalgamated with 48th in 1880 to form the 21st Corps.

48th (Prescott) formed 15 March 1860; attached to 1st Admin. Bn 1863; amalgamated with 47th (St Helens) 1880.

49th (Newton-le-Willows) formed 3 March 1860; attached to 9th Corps 1862; 9th Admin. Bn 1865; consolidated 9th Corps 1880.

50th not formed.

51st (Liverpool) formed 3 March 1860; merged with 72nd (Old Swan) 1862; disappears from Army Lists 1866.

52nd (Dalton) formed from the 37th (Ulverston) 9 April 1861; absorbed into 37B (Barrow) 1870, but Dalton personnel were transferred to 37A (Ulverston) in 1875; part of 5th Admin. Bn.

53rd (Cartmel) formed from the 37th (Ulverston) 9 April 1861; part of 5th Admin. Bn; disappears from Army Lists 1875.

54th (Ormskirk) formed 15 March 1860; attached to 1st Admin. Bn 1863; 1st Corps.

55th (Leigh) formed 3 March 1860; 4th Admin. Bn 1861; consolidated 4th Corps 1880.

56th (Salford) formed 5 March 1860; became 17th Corps 1880.

57th (Ramsbottom) formed 26 March 1860; 3rd Admin. Bn 1861; consolidated 3rd Corps 1880.

58th not formed.

59th (Leyland) formed 29 February 1860; 6th Admin. Bn 1861; consolidated 11th Corps 1880.

60th (Atherton) formed 6 March 1860; 4th Admin. Bn 1861; consolidated 4th Corps 1880.

61st (Chorley) formed 6 March 1860; 6th Admin. Bn 1861; absorbed into 11th (Preston) 1868.

62nd (Clitheroe) formed 27 March 1860; 8th Admin. Bn 1864; consolidated 2nd Corps 1880.

63rd (Toxteth) formed 9 April 1860; 2nd Admin. Bn 1860; part of 5th Lancashire (The Liverpool Rifle Volunteer Brigade) 1862.

64th (Liverpool) formed 25 April 1860, sometimes known as the Liverpool Irish; 2nd Admin. Bn 1861; became 18th Corps 1880.

65th (Rossall) formed February 1860, most of the members were masters and senior boys of Rossall School; 5th Admin. Bn 1863; junior boys' cadet corps formed 1873; converted to Engineer cadets 1890.

66th (Liverpool) formed 25 April 1860; 1st Admin. Bn 1860; part of 1st corps.

67th (Worsley) formed 7 May 1860; 4th Admin. Bn 1860; consolidated 4th Corps 1880.

68th (Liverpool), or Lyceum Corps, formed 31 May 1860; 2nd Admin. Bn 1860; became part of 5th Lancashire (The Liverpool Rifle Volunteer Brigade) 1862.

69th (Liverpool) formed 31 May 1860; 1st Admin. Bn 1860; part of 1st Corps.

70th (Droylesden) formed 5 May 1860; absorbed by the 28th (Manchester) 1862.

71st (Liverpool), sometimes known as Liverpool Highland; 2nd Admin. Bn 1860; became 5th Lancashire (The Liverpool Rifle Volunteer Brigade) 1862.

72nd (Liverpool Old Swan) formed 8 June 1860; absorbed into 51st (Liverpool) 1862.

73rd (Newton) formed 8 June 1860; absorbed by 80th (Liverpool) 1863.

74th (Liverpool St Annes) formed 2 July 1860; absorbed by the 1st (Liverpool) 1862.

75th (Broughton-in-Furness) formed 28 August 1860; 5th Admin. Bn 1861; disbanded 1863.

76th (Farnworth) formed 3 July 1860; 4th Admin. Bn 1860; consolidated 4th Corps 1880.

77th (Widnes) formed 1 October 1860; disbanded 1863.

78th (Manchester) formed 2 November 1860; absorbed by 33rd (Ardwick) 1862.

79th (Liverpool) formed 16 February 1861; absorbed by 5th Lancashire (The Liverpool Rifle Volunteer Brigade) 1862; originally composed of three companies: No. 1 Liverpool Volunteer Guard; No. 2 Great George Ward; No. 3 Lamont's Highland.

80th (Liverpool) formed by the print trade 8 January 1861 and given the additional title 'Press Guard'; became 19th Corps 1880.

81st (Withnell) formed 20 February 1861; 2nd Admin. Bn 1861, then attached 2nd Corps; moved to Wheelton 1864; disbanded 1876.

82nd (Hindley) formed 14 June 1861; amalgamated with 27th (Bolton) 1876.

83rd (Knowsley) formed 11 February 1861; 1st Admin. Bn 1863; absorbed 1876.

84th (Padiham) formed 18 February 1861; 3rd Admin. Bn 1860; consolidated 3rd Corps 1880.

85th not formed.

86th (Liverpool) or Custom's House Corps, formed 18 May 1861; 2nd Admin. Bn 1861; became part of 5th Lancashire (The Liverpool Rifle Volunteer Brigade) 1862.

87th (Nelson) formed 7 February 1862; 3rd Admin. Bn 1862; absorbed 1865.

88th (Haslingden) formed 27 February 1863; 3rd Admin. Bn 1863; consolidated 3rd Corps 1880.

89th not formed.

90th (Fleetwood) formed 3 June 1868; 3rd Admin. Bn 1868; absorbed 1870.

91st (Flixton) formed 14 August 1872; 4th Admin Bn 1872; consolidated 4th Corps 1880.

N.B. Formation dates given are the official acceptance dates or, where this is not known, the date of the first officer's commission in that unit.

Appendix II: The Nominal Rolls 1863–92

The Lancashire Record Office contains a remarkably complete run of nominal rolls from 1863 onward (reference LN 14). They are attested by HM Inspectors beginning with Colonel Bruce, and give the name and parish of each volunteer with the date of enlistment. They give a strong sense of the size and geographical scope of the movement. Most volunteers lived close to their headquarters, but 44th (Longton) LRV must have been unique in that all its members, officers and men, came from the parish of Penwortham in the 1863 roll! The lists are invaluable for genealogists.

Sample data from the 1863 roll are given below.

Unit	Total enrolled	Officer signing return (if signature legible)
1st (Liverpool)	623	Lt Col J. H. Chambers
2nd (Blackburn)	459	Lt Col T. Lund
4th (Stackshead)	71	Lt Col J. Aitken
5th (Liverpool Rifle Brigade)	555	Lt Col R. L. Tilney
6th (Manchester)	783	Lt Col E. Loyd
7th (Accrington)	80	
8th (Bury)	514	Lt Col J. Hutchinson
9th (Warrington)	286	Lt Col J. Greenall
10th (Lancaster)	157	Lt Col H. Gregson
11th (Preston)	281	Major W. Goodair
13th (Southport)	66	Lt Col Heaton-Hesketh
15th (Liverpool)	286	Lt Col T. Browne
17th (Burnley)	145	
21st (Wigan)	139	Capt. N. Eckersley
23rd (Ashton-under-Lyne)	278	Lt Col T. Mellor
24th (Rochdale)	287	Lt Col H. Fishwick
25th (Liverpool)	203	
27th (Bolton)	677	Lt Col Grey
28th (Manchester)	450	
29th (Lytham)	63	Capt. Stevenson

31st (Oldham)	284	Lt Col Blackburne
33rd (Ardwick)	702	Lt Col Cunliffe
37th (Ulverston)	89	Capt. Kennedy
37B (Barrow-in-Furness)	72	J. Ramsden
37C (Hawkshead)	63	
40th (Manchester)	700	Lt Col A. Egerton
42nd (Liverpool)	97	
44th (Longton)	63	
46th (Swinton)	179	J. Dugdale
48th (Prescot)	71	
49th (Newton-le-Willows)	79	J. W. Birley
51st (Liverpool)	623	Lt Col Buckley
52nd (Dalton-in-Furness)	82	
53rd (Cartmel)	68	Halsteade
54th (Ormskirk)	66	W. Welsby
55th (Leigh)	103	Capt. G. Lee
56th (Salford)	437	Capt. T. Heywood
57th (Ramsbottom)	81	
59th (Leyland)	60	
60th (Atherton)	79	Capt. J. P. Fletcher
61st (Chorley)	151	G. H. Lightaller
62nd (Clitheroe)	60	F. Grimshaw
64th (Liverpool)	497	Lt Col P. Bidwell
65th (Rossall)	124	
67th (Worsley)	62	
76th (Farnworth)	68	Lt Col A. Topper
80th (Liverpool)	545	
81st (Withnell)	74	Capt. J. A. Parke
82nd (Hindley)	73	Ensign T. Southworth
83rd (Knowsley)	67	Capt. Whistler
84th (Padiham)	82	
87th (Nelson)	65	Nelson
88th (Haslingden)	90	A. Haworth

1863 grand total LRV	12,456	

Appendix III

The Rifle Volunteer Corps become Volunteer Battalions of Regular Regiments 1881–90

Corps	New Title	Uniform in 1885
1st Corps	became 1st VB The King's (Liverpool) Regiment 1888	Green – black facings
2nd Corps	became 1st VB The East Lancashire Regiment 1889	Scarlet – white facings
3rd Corps	became 2nd VB The East Lancashire Regiment 1889	Scarlet – black facings
4th Corps	became 1st VB The Manchester Regiment 1888	Green – scarlet facings
5th Corps	became 2nd VB The King's (Liverpool) Regiment 1888	Green – scarlet facings
6th Corps	became 2nd VB The Manchester Regiment 1888	Scarlet – yellow facings
7th Corps	became 3rd VB The Manchester Regiment 1880	Scarlet – green facings
8th Corps	became 1st VB The Lancashire Fusiliers 1883	Scarlet – yellow facings
9th Corps	became 1st VB The South Lancashire Regiment 1886	Scarlet – green facings
10th Corps	became 1st VB The King's Own (Royal Lancaster) Regiment 1883	Scarlet – blue facings
11th Corps	became 1st VB The Loyal North Lancashire Regiment 1883	Scarlet – white facings
12th Corps	became 2nd VB The Lancashire Fusiliers 1883	Scarlet – blue facings
13th Corps	became 3rd VB The King's (Liverpool) Regiment 1888	Scarlet – blue facings
14th Corps	became 2nd VB The Loyal North Lancashire Regiment 1887	Scarlet – green facings

The Rifle Volunteer Corps become Volunteer Battalions of Regular Regiments 1881–90

Corps	New Title	Uniform in 1885
15th Corps	became 4th The King's (Liverpool) Regiment 1888	Scarlet – blue facings
16th Corps	became 4th VB The Manchester Regiment 1888	Scarlet – green facings
17th Corps	allotted as a VB of the Manchester Regiment in 1881 but in 1886 became 3rd VB The Lancashire Fusiliers	Scarlet – blue facings
18th Corps	became 5th (Irish) VB The King's (Liverpool) Regiment 1888	Green – scarlet facings
19th Corps	became 6th VB The King's (Liverpool) Regiment 1888	Scarlet – blue facings
20th Corps	became 5th VB The Manchester Regiment 1888	Green – scarlet facings
21st Corps	became 2nd VB The South Lancashire Regiment 1886	Green – scarlet facings
22nd Corps	became 6th VB The Manchester Regiment 1888	Scarlet – green facings
Isle of Man Rifle Volunteers	became attached to 6th VB The King's (Liverpool) Regiment, 1888; sometimes known as 7th (Isle of Man) Volunteer Battalion.	Scarlet – blue facings

Bibliography

There is a huge amount of surviving material on the volunteer movement as a whole; those interested in pursuing the subject beyond Lancashire would be well advised to consult the bibliography in I. F. W. Beckett's *Riflemen Form: a Study of the Rifle Volunteer Movement, 1859–1908* (Ogilby Trusts, 1982). What follows can only be a selection of the sources which have something to contribute to the Lancashire story.

A. Primary sources

Lancashire Record Office, Preston

LA 10 List of commissions in LRV battalions, 1860–74.
LA 11 War Office correspondence concerning LRV appointments and promotions.
LN 14 Nominal rolls of the LRV, 1863–92.
Derbyshire, G., 'Wigan Military Chronicle' (unpublished typescript).

Liverpool Museum

1985.265; 58.83.533 Muster rolls and order books of the Liverpool Rifle Volunteers.

Liverpool Scottish Museum

Orderly Books, 1860s.
Shooting Records, 1860s.

Manchester Central Library

MS 356 14 M3 Notes on the Manchester Volunteer Battalions.

Public Record Office, Kew

PRO WO 13 Payments to volunteer units.

Rossall School Archives

B ms 10. 65th (Rossall) LRV muster roll.
B ms 11. 65th (Rossall) LRV formation and early history.

South Lancashire Regiment Museum

Scrapbook of the 9th (Warrington) LRV in two volumes, 1865–79 and 1879–89.

B. Newspapers

Fleetwood Chronicle
Manchester Guardian

C. Secondary sources

A Short History of the Volunteer Movement in Bolton (Bolton, 1880).

Axon., W. E. A., *The Annals of Manchester: a Chronological Record from the Earliest Times to the End of 1885* (Heywood, 1886).

Beckett, I. F. W., *Riflemen Form: a Study of the Rifle Volunteer Movement, 1859–1908* (Ogilby Trusts, 1982).

ᴾ., *A History of the Formation and Development of the Volunteer Infantry ‹arliest Times, Illustrated by the Local Records of Huddersfield and its ›om 1794 to 1874* (Simpkin, Marshall & Co., 1903).

he Rifle and How to Use It (G. Routledge, 1958).

L. M., *Altcar, the Story of a Rifle Range* (Territorial, Auxiliary ..unteer Reserve Assoc., 1989).

Cornfield, S., *The Queen's Prize: the Story of the National Rifle Association* (Pelham, 1987).

Cousins, G., *The Defenders: a History of the British Volunteer* (Muller, 1968).

Cowper, L. I., *The King's Own: the Story of a Royal Regiment*, 3 vols (vols 1 and 2, O.U.P., 1937; vol. 3, Gale and Polton, 1957).

Crompton, W., and Venn, G., *Warrington Volunteers, 1798–1898* (Sunrise Pub., 1898).

Durham, W., *Blackburn, Lancashire: Chronological Notes on the History of the Town and Parish of Blackburn from AD 317 to AD 1861 . . .* (Charles Tiplady, 1866).

Edwards, D., and Langley, D., *British Army Proficiency Badges* (Wardley, 1984).

Fell, A., *Furness Military Chronicle* (Kitchin, 1937).

The First Manchester Rifle Volunteers Grand Military Bazaar (Manchester, 1884).

French, J. D., *A History of Altcar Rifle Range* (West Lancashire Territorial and Auxiliary Force, 1961).

Hayhurst, T. H., *A History and some Records of the Volunteer Movement in Bury, Heywood, Rossendale, and Ramsbottom* (T. Crompton, 1887).

Hewitson, A., *History of Preston in the County of Lancaster* (Preston Chronicle, 1883).

Kipling, A. L., and King, H. L., *Headdress Badges of the British Army*, vol. 1 (Muller, 1978).

Peters, H., *Fleetwood and the Military Connexion* (unpub. thesis in Fleetwood library, [1976]).

Roads, G. H., *The British Soldier's Firearm, 1850–1864* (Jenkins, 1964).

Rose, R. B., 'Liverpool Volunteers of 1859' in *The Liverpool Bulletin*, October, 1956.

— 'The Volunteers of 1859' in *Journal of the Society of Army Historical Research*, 1959.

Rules and Regulations of the Liverpool Scottish Rifle Volunteers (Liverpool, 1860).

Temple, B. A., and Skennerton, I. D., *A Treatise on the British Military Martini: Henry, 1869–c. 1900* (Australia, B. A. Temple, 1983).

War Office, *Army Lists, 1859–85*.

— *Regulations for the Volunteer Force* (1863, 1878 and 1881).

Westlake, R., *The Volunteer Infantry, 1880–1908* (Military History Soc., 1992).

— *The Rifle Volunteers* (Picton, 1982).

— *The Territorial Battalions: a Pictorial History, 1859–1985* (Spellmount, 1986).

Wilkinson, H. A., *Citizen Soldiers: Essays Towards the Improvement of the Volunteer Force* (Kegan Paul, 1884).

Wyatt, R. J., *Collecting Volunteer Militaria* (David & Charles, 1974).

Wylly, H. C., *The Loyal North Lancashire Regiment*, 2 vols. (Royal United Services Institution, 1933).